I will not surrender to terrorism

Gijo Vijayan

ISBN: 1535453052
ISBN-13: 978-1535453059

DEDICATION

This book is dedicated to misguided youth worldwide who joined various terror organizations due to brainwashing of various ideologies. A humble attempt is made to bring them back to normal life through this book. Even if one person is converted because of this book, the goal of this book is achieved. Stay away from terrorism, it is the number one enemy of Humanity. Use your common sense Now.

This book is also dedicated to lives lost in the mindless acts of terrorism worldwide. May their souls rest in peace. AMEN.

CONTENTS

Mass re-education of politicians around the world.

Why People think, my god is better than your god?

We need Anti-terror universities:

Glorification of terrorism:

Why people get mad over ideology?

Even distribution of resources is the best anti-dot for terrorism.

What is the best way to prevent terrorism?

Role of education in preventing terrorism:

What is the best thing about China?

Relation between terrorism and food habits:

Justification of war in the name of terrorism.

Private terrorism – a Big industry now:

Know the truth about terrorism – You will never be a terrorist.

How to eliminate terror organizations that cause harm to the world?

Intelligence Gathering – Key to kill Terrorism

Racial tension, one of the main causes of terrorism:

Overpopulation is the root cause of all evils in this world:

Responsibility of youth – One child policy or No Child policy:

Meat Consumption.

Throw away gold and diamonds:

Conclusion.

Gijo Vijayan

ACKNOWLEDGMENTS

I am indebted to my brother **Mr.S** and family for providing all moral and material support to complete this book. The contents of this book is brief, so you can understand and get the message fast and easy. This book is deliberately written short to save your time.

Chapter 1

DONOT SPOIL YOUR PRECIOUS LIFE.

Use your common sense, do not become a terrorist and spoil your life. Persuade people who follow terrorism and turn them off from the wrong path. If you can control your mind, you can control terrorism. The mindset that create a terror ideology is, I am always right, others are wrong and they do not have right to exist.

Just think that, like you exist, every living being on earth has also the right to exist even though they do not believe in what you believe or look like how you look, or think like how you think. Live and let Live, terrorism will end.

Insert chapter one text here. Insert chapter one text here. Insert chapter one text here. Insert chapter one text here. Insert chapter one text here. Insert chapter one text here.

Chapter 2

AIM OF THIS BOOK

This book aims at preventing a person from becoming a terrorist. The author aim at killing the motive behind terrorism, whatever may be the reason behind. Forgive and forget, the world will be safer. An eye for an eye make the whole world blind, said Mahatma Gandhi.

If you know anyone, who has extreme and radical views on religion or any ideology, that cause harm to society. This book can be an eye opener to narrow minded people, who think I am right and whole world is wrong.

Stop revenge, forgive and forget, the world will be safer. For nations to live in peace, stop quest for dominance, stop trying to grab someone's land or sea. More investment in military makes common people suffer indirectly. Billions of dollars spent on military expenses can be diverted for betterment of the lives of people, if there is no friction between nations.

Billions of dollars spent on atom bombs, missiles, ships, fighter planes etc will eventually of no use to the betterment of humanity. If a third world war occurs, there won't be anyone left to celebrate victory, so it is foolishness to wage war in the name of any ideology or religion.

There is only One way to stop terrorism – Education.

When millions of people refuse to become terrorist at any cost – by applying thought, the purpose of this book is achieved.

To kill terrorism, we must kill the motivation behind terrorism. When you refuse to become a terrorist, you make the world safer. When millions of people around the world refuse to become terrorists, we all win.

So, take a pledge today itself

- I will not become a terrorist

- I will not allow my kids to become terrorists

- I will not change my mind, because of people or circumstances around me

- No media , politics or religion can manipulate me

- I will help misguided people to leave the path of terrorism

Chapter 3

POOR UNDERSTANDING ABOUT
CONCEPT OF GOD

Poor understanding about god is the biggest reason for terrorism. The simple thought that motivates every religious terrorist is that my god is better than your god, my religion is better than your religion.

Major religions worldwide have failed to convey to people that god is one and there is Gods can't be branded through religion.
Branding god using religion is the starting point of terrorism.

Religions are path to reach gods, but now days, it has become the perfect path to promote violence and terrorism by politicians to retain   power.

When you cement the following idea in your mind, you genuinely know God HINDU GOD Equals MUSLIM God Equals CHRISTIAN GOD Equals Buddhist God Equals any other Branded God = ONE GOD. All is one.

If you think that my god is better than any other god from any religion, you must call yourself a live terrorist and need serious mental treatment. This distorted thinking must be killed using logic.

How to kill terrorism?

• Distance yourself from religion motivated political forces

• Think about yourself

• Never support , propagate or practice any violent ideology

• Do not brand a religion or community because of few terrorists.

• Never develop your own opinion based on manipulated mass

media, social media etc, make your own judgment.

- Try to find out what happened to people who chose path of terrorism to achieve their goals.

- Ensure you never get provoked by religious and race ideologies.

- Stop wearing religious symbols; nobody must be able to make out your religion, just by seeing you.

- Always remember that terrorism is the enemy of Humanity.

Chapter 4

WHAT IS THE FUTURE OF A TERRORIST ?
ANSWER = DEATH

If you are a motivated terrorist, this book will help you to become a Normal Person. Death is waiting the terrorist. Do not surrender your mind to any ideology that causes harm to your fellow human beings.

Terrorists are created, through ideological brainwashing for political purpose. Terrorists are pawns in the hands of politicians.

Terrorists finally get killed for no reason.

A branded terrorist bring shame to community and religion he represents and entire community is affected.

Terrorism causes deep division in society and leads to fear psychosis. Terrorism is the enemy of Humanity.

Chapter 5

HOW TO KILL TERRORISM USING EDUCATION?

The best tool to kill terrorism is through education. A child must never be ideologically motivated by any religion at any cost because, he can become a future terrorist. What every religious fanatic teach kids ? that my religion is best, those who do not believe in my religion, do not have the right to exist. I have the right to kill them.

Infuse this idea into the head of any kid before the age of 10, he may naturally become a terrorist who can be manipulated by politicians and media to retain power.

Every kid must learn about other religion and learn to respect other's faith and way of life. When you develop respect for each other's religion, it not only kill terrorism, but also enable better understanding between people.

When a person has clear understanding about every religion, he can never become a terrorist. Even if a terror attack happens to him, he will think that terrorists are bad people and will not blame his neighbor who belongs to that religion. A properly educated kid about terrorism can never be lured into religious terrorism because he know the consequences.

Chapter 6

JUST APPLY THIS SIMPLE LOGIC

I am a Christian because I was born to Christian Parents, I did not choose my name or religion at the time of my birth, everything has been thrust upon me by society. So, How can I say that my religion is best and only Jesus Christ is right, every other religion is nonsense and people of other faith do not have right to exist ?

If you apply common sense, you will keep away from ideologies that make you a terrorist.

Chapter 7

IF GOD COULD SPEAK TO A HARDCORE RELIGIOUS TERRORIST ?

Imagine if god happen to meet a hardcore terrorist and speak to him ? He/ She may then commit suicide thinking about the folly for which they are fighting for. Following is the interview between god and a hardcore terrorist:

God: What you are doing here?

Terrorist: I am here to protect your name and rule on earth, non believers are not following you.

God: I created you , this earth and billions of stars and this universe , I don't need your protection.

Terrorist: I know that , I respect that. But others are misusing your name and commit sins.

God: Do not worry, I will deal with their sins.

Terrorist: No, I will deal with them, I being your servant, I can't see non-believers misusing your name using another religion.

God: Dear Son, other people following other religions are also worshipping me, your god and their god is same, myself.

Terrorist: No never, that is not what I have been told or taught in my school. My god is real god, all other gods and religions are false, they do not have the right to exist. We will cleanse all these false worshippers and make this earth paradise. Only my god is true god.

God: Son, who taught you this? It must be Satan. You know I created Satan so that people know me, think about me during their difficult times.

Terrorist: Dear god, we have branded you, built large worshipping centers for you around the world, millions of people pray to you every day, only my god is real, nothing else is real.

God: Son, you are confused, people who do not belong to your religion also worship me, I am the same god you also worship. Please understand.

Terrorist: No never, false gods others worship, some worship stones, monkeys, sun, rivers, what a foolishness.

God: Son , they see me in those objects and imagine about me, through these images, there is nothing wrong with it.

Terrorist: Hell No, I object is, only my way of seeing you dear god is perfect and all others are fools, please make them understand.

God: My son, I tried my best to convince you, people who do not belong to your religion worship me only, they may look different, but they think about me only.

Terrorist: Sorry, I don't believe it, only my god is real, what I think is correct, I will eliminate all these fake worshippers and establish paradise on earth.

God: Son, you are wrong, don't do it.

Terrorist: I am going to tell them, join my religion or die…………

God: Son, please don't do that, you may get killed instead and people from other religions will think that all people who belong to your religion are terrorists.

Terrorist: That is not a problem; I will establish your world here at any cost even if I die.

God: Dear son, now nobody can save you. You are under the grip of Satan.

The following day, there was a massive suicide attack by terrorist on non-believers and more than hundred people got killed in an airport. It included many women and kids.

The souls of all those killed including the terrorist reach god. Then god began to speak.

God: Dear Son, why did you kill these innocent people, they did no harm to you.

Terrorist: No, they were worshippers of false gods, they deserved to die.

God: Son, you totally destroyed my calculations

Terrorist: I am sure , now you will grand me paradise.

God: Hell No, you are going to burn in hell for millions of years, also take over the sins of innocent people who died because of you.

Terrorist: That is not fair my god, I worked hard to protect your name and follow you truly, I deserve paradise. These people deserve hell, as they are not true believers.

God: No never, I am pushing you to hell, burn there now.

Soon terrorist was pushed into hell by god and before he could repent, the hell fire started gulping him.

Chapter 8

WHO CREATE TERRORISTS?

Terrorists are created by vested interests and politicians to wield power. They brainwash the followers in the name of religion and political ideology. They brainwash them and use them as cannon fodders to achieve their political goals.

Enemy countries fund, support and create terrorists in other countries to subjugate a nation politically and economically. Terrorists are funded and abetted by vested interests for political gains, mixing religion to it makes it more potent weapon.

Terror organizations are also created by companies that want to sell their weapons. Create fear, sell weapons. This is a tactic used by people who sell arms.

Chapter 9

WILL REVENGE WORK?

Imagine someone did something bad to you. You are innocent, you need not take revenge on your enemy, leave it to god. No one can escape law of Karma. When worms are alive, we catch them and use it to catch fish, and eat it. But when we die, the worms will eat us. It is only a question of time, that those who did bad to us will suffer. Just wait and watch silently.

One of the major reason given by terrorist is quest for revenge and subjugation of its people. But gun won't solve any problem, more terrorists get killed every day due to quest for revenge. If you decide not to take revenge on people who did bad to you or your family, god will forgive you and punish the sinners. If you take revenge, someone will again take renege on you and this cycle can repeat unlimited, causing death and destruction.

Chapter 10

TERRORISM AND FREEDOM STRUGGLE
THE THIN LINE

Many terrorists all over the world disguise as freedom fighters. They have their own reason for that. How to disguise terrorists and freedom fighters ? It is very simple. If people of every community , every religion fight together hand in hand to set free from tyranny or oppressed rule for a just cause, it can be termed as freedom fighting. There is a justification for that. Indian freedom struggle from Britain is the classic example. All people, communities fought alongside like brothers to attain freedom.

Terrorism is nasty. It is the act of a group of criminals who kill, loot and destroy property of its enemy including the common people, innocent people without any valid reason. Their acts have no solid political aim but to create fear in the minds of people and control them. Terrorism is blind to justice, freedom struggle is not. You must use your brain and study history before concluding whether a struggle is freedom struggle or terrorism. A selective one sided violent attack can never be termed as freedom struggle.

Chapter 11

HOW TERRORIST'S MIND WORK?

A terrorist need not be a gun wielding person going around and killing people. You can describe anyone with a brain washed mind, who refuse to accept the truth and look at things with a bias in mind, without using logic can be termed as terrorist. There is no place in his mind for logic or reasoning, what I believe is 100% right, everyone else is totally wrong. He sees only injustice and attack on his people and blind to people who don't belong to his ideology, race or religion. For a terrorist, anyone who do not support him is his enemy.

A terrorist hate anyone based on predetermined parameters set in his mind. It can be religious, racial or ideological. You can simply call someone whose 50% brain is almost dead as terrorist.

Once people are hallucinated using an ideology and they become hardened, the vested interests use them as pawns to achieve their goals. Terrorists get eliminated during the course of military action or get killed by rivals in the long term.

Chapter 12

WHICH BRAND OF GOD IS BETTER?

Can you answer this question, which god is better?

Hindu God

Muslim God

Christian God

Buddhist God

Other Gods

The simple answer to this is – all gods are one, you call them by different names.

You need not have to project your god, no need to preach or show to others that your god is better and more powerful that other gods. You need to develop wisdom for this.

You can understand this by simple logic. Collect water from Russia, America, China, India, Nigeria, Brazil, Australia from rivers. Test in a lab and find out if there is any difference. It is same H_2O everywhere. So, also god, we call it by different names. **But all is one, One is all. Universal brotherhood is impossible without real understanding of god.**

Chapter 13

THE STARTING POINT OF CONFLICT SEGREGATION

The biggest reason for war in future will start from Religion. In the past religion has been a great unifying force, but now no more. Religion will be the biggest and single most reason for war in future. Today millions of people across the world wear religious symbols, which segregate them from the rest, this is the starting point of war.

More individuals form community conclaves and pit against each other based on religious beliefs. Nations will get divided based on religion and it can trigger war. It is only a question of time.

Chapter 14

HOW TO PREVENT RELIGIOUS WAR?

Please do not wear religious symbols in public.

Do not get brainwashed by religious and political leaders

Do not get tensed or emotional on hearing something had happened bad to people belonging to your community or religion, think about the suffering people.

As far as possible avoid taking part in rituals and ceremonies relating to religion as show of strength. Keep it a private affair.

Do not contribute money time or material to radical religious organizations that preach hate, nor allow your kids to go near the same.

Do not make fun of other people's religion, no matter how foolish it may occur to you.

Chapter 15

WHO CREATE WARS WORLDWIDE?

Have you ever wondered, why so many conflicts are going on across the world and so many people are getting killed every day? Why is it happening? The reason is simple, individuals have become violent, there is no harmony inside self, so no peace in society and people turn violent for simple reasons. There is no tolerance limit.

Another reason for more conflicts is the ever growing population of countries. More people , less resources and fight to capture resources. There is only one way to balance world population.

Let the youth of the world decide, they won't produce kids for a generation, the world population will come down. Let it be a mass movement. Less population means, less people to fight wars and die, more land to cultivate. Happier life. More we burden the earth with people, nature will automatically eliminate us by creating disease, wars or by natural calamities, the big disasters are waiting to happen.

One of the major creators of wars worldwide are corporations that manufacture weapons. They create terror organizations, fund them and create violence. Fear will prompt countries to buy more weapons. To keep the weapon sales high, it is necessary to create enmity between nations. If nations are tolerant, we actually do not need armed forces. But that will never happen.

It is the quest for power among the powerful nations that make them invest millions of dollars in arms and defense modernization. When a country invests more money in defense, it is the common man who suffers.

The money that is to be utilized for building roads, hospitals, healthcare and pension for the old is utilized for war. Few companies and individuals get rich day by day at the cost of millions of poor people.

Every country wants to dominate other country, grab land and project as power. This is the reason for world poverty. The moment the enemy is weak, the opponent will attack him. This fear psychosis force countries to invest in weapons of future. As a result the world has enough weapons of mass destruction to destroy the earth completely several times.

Greed for power has caused situations. Many people in Asia and Africa do not have enough to eat but they have weapons to fight and die for no reason.

Wars are created to divert attention of people of a specific country that is undergoing turmoil. Politicians use patriotism as a weapon to justify war. Legacy can be another reason for war, thousands of years back, that piece of land belonged to our ancestors, we need to recover that, so we have to go for war. This can be one of the reasons for future wars. Patriotism and Jingoism can be one of the biggest sources of war in the coming days.

Chapter 16

WHY WAR IS INEVITABLE IN FUTURE?

Wars will happen between nations in future, no one can stop it. More fights between individuals also will happen because, people are greedy , adamant and selfish. Religion and education has failed to provide them happiness and people are becoming wild day by day. Compare with people living 100 years ago and now in any part of the world, there is less compassion, tolerance now that those times, among people. The diminishing love between people is the main reason for war.

Every country want to dominate each other, every religion want to dominate each other, every race of people want to dominate one another, then how can peace ever exist ? It seems impossible. Mutually assured total destruction only will be able to prevent wars of future.

Chapter 17

WHAT CAN PREVENT FUTURE WARS?

Most of the nations of the world, big or small is today being ruled directly or indirectly by a group of lunatic people (Oligarchs) who never care about opinion of the society. They manipulate media, religion, press etc and invent situations that keep them in power.

Ironically it is the weapons of mass destruction and technology that will prevent future wars. Mutually assured total destruction will force nations to think hundred times before launching missiles or nuclear weapons. To win while sitting across the negotiation table, one need to show military power, that is why most rival countries develop more destructive weapons.

To make world safer, this balance of power is very much needed. Weapons of mass destructions will be doves of peace in the coming days. Nothing else is going to work.

You can bring an enemy to its heals and make them obey your terms using

Military Superiority

Technology Superiority

Economic Power

To sympathy or compassion like Gandhi model will work in the 21st century. People who resort to non-violent methods of agitation will be isolated and brutally killed by fanatical regimes and religious groups. Only weapons and power will work, along with diplomacy that will bring lasting peace in the world.

Chapter 18

MASS RE-EDUCATION OF POLITICIANS AROUND THE WORLD.

Even if this is a futile attempt, we must try it out. Politicians control nations, If they happen to be good, we have better chance of peace. Most of the politicians around the world now seems to work like agents of satan rather than agent of god. If we had good politicians, we can bring peace between nations. In political race everywhere, we see bad people win over the good ones.

If we have a university to teach politicians the values of peace and perils of war, we may see some change in the world. Good leaders will prevent war while evil politicians will create war for their own benefits. But chances of occurrence of massive nuclear war worldwide is very dim, because no country want to die completely and there won't be any clear winner in future.

Chapter 19

WHY PEOPLE THINK, MY GOD IS BETTER THAN YOUR GOD?

This happens due to poor education and ignorance. If wrong information is pumped into your head right from childhood that only your religion , way of life and your god is true god, all others are false and stupid, then that personal can naturally become a supporter of terrorism or terrorist himself.

His view of the world is singular and narrow minded. He can view the people and world around him through the prism of religious belief only. This is the starting point of segregation that eventually lead to segregation of societies. The mere sight of anyone who is not like him, make the individual uncomfortable. This is the true reason for religious war.

When many people think like what is said above, there is a big problem that will arise in future. It is a very dangerous trend. We need to discourage people from making a narrow interpretation of religion.

Chapter 20

WE NEED ANTI-TERROR UNIVERSITIES.

I feel that we may need anti-terror universities all over the world to prevent terrorism and reduce the effect of terrorism. The curriculum must contain studies on how not to become a violent terrorist.

This is very helpful in converting minds of students who become radical due to the influence of radical ideologies around the globe. Instead of killing a terrorist after he actually become one, we need to kill the factors and thoughts that mould and nurture a terrorist right from the Childhood.

Chapter 21

GLORIFICATION OF TERRORISM.

Violence begets violence, no problem in this world was ever solved by guns, what can work out is negotiation. Motivation to become a terrorist can be many, but eventually the person get killed in armed action, more terrorists are brainwashed and more of them will be killed , if there is armed action.

Politicians use glorification of dead terrorists to motivate young men to join terror organization, also offer them money and women. Thousands of young men are dead already who chose the wrong paths of terrorism, more will die in future, those who are following the wrong path

Chapter 22

WHY PEOPLE GET MAD OVER IDEOLOGY?

The biggest threat to world peace today is closed minds of people. The ideology brainwash people so much that they begin to think that nothing is above the ideology I think, nothing must exist above that and anyone who opposes my way of thinking must be eliminated.

The thinking of leaders of many countries are also not different. My country, my people, my race and my political system must dominate the world and I will use my country's military might to crush anything that comes on my way. This mindset of leaders transfer to masses and create an atmosphere of Patriotism and jingoism which is the starting point of war. Former dictator of Germany, Hitler is the classic example.

Do not allow yourself to be brain dead, do not close your brain to truth. Please do not think that when you close the eye, the whole world is dark. Have mercy on poor people, suffering people, the real victims of war and terrorism and people suffering from poverty due to over expenditure of military in a country. The hard mindset of leaders prevent homogeneous distribution of wealth in the society. More emphasis is laid on military and non productive things to control power, as a result a section of the society suffer a lot and get sidelined. They are denied economic rights and right of a decent living.

Have you ever thought, why so many people are living in poverty even though we have abundant of food resources worldwide. The answer is greed. Greed of the political leaders create poverty. Money that is to be used for making roads, bridges and other infrastructure is spent on military in billions of dollars. One of the reasons for poverty in many African countries is over spending on military and less focus on agriculture, because of which people do not have enough to eat, but they have more guns to fire.

Chapter 23

EVEN DISTRIBUTION OF RESOURCES IS THE BEST ANTIDOTE FOR TERRORISM.

Denial is the biggest source of terrorism worldwide, other than religious terrorism. When a society is denied its basic need and right to exist, life becomes hard. The common man has to toil a lot to make a living and also fight with insecurity and corruption.

The single biggest factor that can prevent mass uprising is availability of food materials in abundance at low prices. If you study the root cause of many world revolutions, it actually started from denial of food. Make food available to people in cheap and plenty, the common man will be happy.

In any country, if the food prices are high, people will be unhappy and it can even lead to civil war. In this world of acute denial and imbalance of wealth between people, what prevents the poor people from murdering the rich is faith in god. Here religion plays an important role.

The wide income gap between the rich and poor is one of the major cause of concern in any society. One of the weakness of Capitalism is massive accumulation of wealth in the hands of few individuals while millions of people struggle to make both ends meet every day. India, China, Brazil and America are the best examples before your eyes.

Chapter 24

WHAT IS THE BEST WAY TO PREVENT TERRORISM?

If any government make the life of common man easy, that country will progress fast. The common man must be able to afford food, shelter, clothing, education and security at less cost. Singapore is a classic example of excellent governance in spite of having almost ZERO resources. The government of Singapore love its people so much, that they ensure there is clean environment, fast access to justice, education, health and economic opportunity.

The streets are clean and no filth anywhere, strict action will be taken against any corrupt person or civil servant, also if you break traffic rules or commit any offence, the penalty is high. A very smart and proactive government who really care about its people can prevent the rise of terrorism.

When people are discontented due to denial of basic rights, terrorism starts and it can even lead to mass riots and civil war.

Chapter 25

ROLE OF EDUCATION IN PREVENTING TERRORISM.

If you look at the world today, you can emulate three countries which has risen only due to excellent education. They are Finland, Japan and Singapore, Denmark. In these countries, education is excellent, cheap and available to common man at low cost and quality. Right from childhood, the education system is so well crafted that, anyone who has undergone education in these countries right from birth, can seldom become a terrorist. They make excellent individuals out of education who concentrate on science and technology.

The per capita incomes of these countries are so high that, the common man is able to fulfill all basic needs with less effort. In these countries, you find low unemployment rate and government is helping the youth with programs to rise fast in life. The mind of the youth is focused on economic goals rather than on any foolish ideology that causes destruction.

Chapter 26

WHAT IS THE BEST THING ABOUT CHINA?

Communist ideology has many weakness , it leads to tyranny and ruthlessly crush anything that it feels threatened, There is no freedom of press nor the people have voting rights. But there is one good thing about China which can be a role model to countries worldwide. There is no inflation in China past 25 years. That means the food prices have not changed much last 25 years. As soon as commodity prices go up, the government intervenes and control the same and take strict action on speculators.

If you travel all over China, you find food is available at low price, in abundance. This is the root cause of the mere existence of communist party. Any government that gives it people cheap and nutritious food will be able to stay in power for long. This is what China teach us. If food prices go up, there will be unrest in the society and it can even lead to civil war.

Chapter 27

RELATION BETWEEN TERRORISM AND FOOD HABITS.

The food we consume is spent as three parts. Body absorbs the nutrients, excreta goes out and it controls mind. So, if you want to change your mind, the most important step is to control the food habits. A person who consume meat regularly develops animal like instincts. This is a proven fact. His sex urge will be higher. A person who consume meat and meat products regularly can easily kill another human being without much emotion attached to it, in the event of a conflict. The mind of a terrorist is very much influenced by his food habits.

A society that is predominantly non-vegetarian will be violent by nature. It can be violent individuals at home or in workplace. The animal hormones and content will affect his thinking to a great extent. The body also will be prone to diseases in course of time. If you want to understand the concept better, do the following experiment.

Allow a group of hardcore terrorists and criminals to eat only vegetarian food over a period of two years and allow them to do farming. I am sure, after 2 years of this exercise, we get a completely transformed individual. Food affects the mind, science has proved the same. Many religious texts says so. You can refer if you want.

Watch closely a society that is mostly vegetarian and Non-Vegetarian, you will find that the Non-Vegetarian society is more violent and aggressive. In the ancient past, India had a very rich culture and tradition of food. We were a vegetarian society. There was almost no crime and poverty. People had high intellect and they produced excellent thinkers, scientists, artists, writers, philosophers, mathematicians etc. One of the reason for this high intelligence is non polluted vegetarian food. Stop meat and all non –vegetarian food to a country that is violent, in course of time, they will mellow down. More meat and meat products you eat, more bloodier you become.

Chapter 28

JUSTIFICATION OF WAR IN THE NAME OF TERRORISM.

The biggest justification and cause of war worldwide is due to terrorism. When you decrease the possibility of terrorism, you decrease the possibility of war so that peace will prevail. The biggest war in middle east started after September 9/11 , 2001 attack occurred in America where 3000 people were killed. Pakistan and India came close to war after major terror attacks like Mumbai attack. Terrorism is like the pin of a grenade, remove the pin and grenade will explode.

There are several instances in the history where war started after terror attack. Hundreds of terror attacks on the soil of Israel forced it to retaliate on its enemies in a brutal manner causing heavy death and destruction. Countries use the justification of terrorism to wage war worldwide, but actually more common people get killed in war, the classic example being Iraq and Afghanistan. By killing the cause that create a terrorist, we not only eliminate terrorism, but also save lives of millions of people, who may die in war later. War will only help arms making companies to thrive and common man will suffer everywhere.

A war monger is looking for creating war so that he can flex his muscle and control politics, people and nation, also give escape route of politicians who failed to perform. By becoming a terrorist, you must not fall into the trap of politicians and religious leaders who use terrorists as cannon fodder to meet their political and material ends.

Chapter 29

PRIVATE TERRORISM – A BIG INDUSTRY NOW.

All over the world terror organizations are nurtured , funded, aided and abetted by powerful governments and political class to bring down the enemy. There are only few ideologically motivated terrorists in this world, compared to those who are fighting for money.

Because of this single factor funded terrorism will never end, the main cause of funded terrorism becoming successful is poverty. After suffering acute poverty people are ready to do anything for money, including taking part in militia. In many African countries, you can start an armed militia just for 500 US dollars. Private militias also raised by drug mafia especially in Latin American countries to protect drug trade.

In many cases a smaller country uses terrorism as a state policy to attack a bigger country by forming private militia and engage in guerilla warfare. The members of guerilla warfare eventually get killed by the military in armed action. The smaller country do not have the military capability to take on to the larger country and they use guerilla warfare as a state policy. This is called state sponsored terrorism. This is what exactly Pakistan is doing to India from 1988 in Kashmir. But Indian military is so vast and capable that it can nullify the effect of state sponsored terrorism at the cost of the state.

Chapter 30

KNOW THE TRUTH ABOUT TERRORISM – YOU WILL NEVER BE A TERRORIST.

If you really know the trust about terrorism and the motive behind it, you will never become a terrorist. Just think, why you get killed for stupid reasons? to fulfill someone's political and economical goal ? Imagine how many young men have died in the past becoming terrorist and no use to anyone. Do you want to get killed like them for stupid reasons? Is your life valuable? Just think, before becoming a terrorist and taking up guns. Think 100 times before you take up gun. Once you take up gun, the whole world will brand you as terrorist. There will be an invisible bullet always chasing to take your precious life away and it will happen sooner or later. The more famous terrorist you become, more guns will be chasing you.

Just before taking up guns, just look around and see the person or leader who motivate young men and women to take up guns. You won't find their kids as terrorist. Most of the terrorist leaders ensure that their family and kids are well protected and lead a luxurious life elsewhere may be even in foreign countries. The leader will never use his sons and daughters as cannon fodders to achieve political and economic goals. If you ask the terrorism promoting leaders, why their kids are not fighting, you can even get killed also. This is the truth about many terrorist organizations.

In any terror organization, they never call themselves as terrorists, but freedom fighters. The whole world may brand them as terrorists, but those who are fighting call themselves as freedom fighters. This is the truth about terrorism.

Chapter 31

HOW TO ELIMINATE TERROR ORGANIZATIONS THAT CAUSE HARM TO THE WORLD?

1.Kill the ideology that motivate people to take up terrorism

To eliminate terrorism, we need to eliminate the root cause that make people terrorist. The ideology of hate must be cut down, whether it emanate from religion or any other isms. Once someone is ideologically motivated and take up terrorism as a means to achieve political and economic goals, then until when that person is killed, the terrorism in him won't die. Heroic deeds of terrorists motivate others to take up terrorism and follow the path of destruction. Terrorism is like a pestilence, it destroy whatever it touches. Only education and counseling of society can help to overcome this problem.

2.Hunt down and kill leaders who make people terrorists

Many funded terror organizations die a natural death, when the leaders are killed. Killing the leaders will split the organization and a leaderless organization will naturally die down. There are many examples of the same for the above.

3.Penetrate into terror organizations and destroy it

The best way to destroy mafia like terror organizations is to penetrate into it and then destroy it from within. This is a tough task, but it can break the back bone of any organization anywhere in the world. As soon as secrets of the organizations are leaked outside, it becomes weak and its leaders will be on the run. If you study, how Italian Police destroyed many mafia organizations, you will get classic examples of the same.

4.Cure terrorism from beginning; eliminate discontent and imbalance in society.

If a section of people are unhappy and are denied economical and other resources and opportunities, government must come into picture and fulfill the gap. Once imbalance in the society is addressed, terrorism will die. Acute poverty can lead to mass rebellion. In such places food must bust made available in plenty and cheap at subsidized rates. Fulfill the common man's need, food, shelter and clothing, rest all will be ok.

Chapter 32

INTELLIGENCE GATHERING – KEY TO KILL TERRORISM.

America is one country that spends billions of dollars on intelligence gathering. Information is the key to war also our fight against terrorism will not be complete without strong intelligence reports.

Terrorism is the enemy of humanity, we need to kill it at any cost, Innocent men and women are killed worldwide due to the mindless acts of terrorists across the world. No one is safe today, even in a pub terror attack can happen that can take away your life. Recent terror attacks in Belgium, USA, France , India are the classic examples. The countries must be sincere in eliminating terrorism. There is nothing called good terrorism and bad terrorism. The curse of humanity are those countries that are supporting and opposing terrorism simultaneously.

Chapter 33

RACIAL TENSION, ONE OF THE MAIN CAUSES OF TERRORISM.

In many parts of the world, the racial tensions are high. Different races of people refuse to mix or mingle causing divide right from birth to death. When economic opportunities are denied to people of a specific race, tension starts. The mall shootings across the world are frustrated individuals who may be victims of racial divide, who may want to give collective punishment. Several racially motivated crimes in America are the best examples. Unless the complete society undergoes transformation, we can't do anything about it. Race and religion as mix is deadlier than RDX now days. It is the biggest dividing factor dividing humanity instead of integrating.

My skin is better than your skin attitude is the biggest satanic thinking in this world, you can't control anyone's skin. The thickness of your skin pigment is only few microns deep (1 micron = 1/1000th of a millimeter). You have no right to discriminate or judge anyone looking at his skin color, but the people refuse to change. Millions of people from Africa were used as slaves in the past in Europe and America. This is the biggest act of crime against humanity. Look at Brain, not at skin color is the advice from the author of this book.

It is hard to change a person with extreme racial attitude. If you live in such a society that humiliate you every day and deny you economic opportunity, the best option is to settle somewhere else.

Chapter 34

OVERPOPULATION IS THE ROOT CAUSE OF ALL EVILS IN THIS WORLD.

The problems in this world are increasing day by day. The root cause of the evil is over population. The population of earth is over 7 billion people, it is increasing day by day. More mouths needed to be fed, need shelter and clothing. Forests are being cut down and environment is getting destroyed. Terrorism is rising. There is struggle for grabbing resources everywhere. The earth's minerals are exploited like never before due to greed. It may look funny and foolish. One of the best way to reduce problems in the world is not to produce further people. If one generation in all the countries decide, they don't produce kids, the world population will come down drastically. There won't be so much fight for resources including food, everyone will have enough.

We need a massive movement to reduce the world population. You need to make independent decision; I won't burden this earth by bringing another person. When millions of people around the world do so, there will be great impact on world population. Even in war, there will be only few people to fight and die also. Less population means plenty of food available, there won't be anyone suffering from poverty anywhere in the world. On the other hand, imagine if people start having 5 to 10 kids, then over a period of 50 to 100 years, our earth will get destroyed, or nature will destroy humanity using disease or natural calamity.

Overpopulation is a very serious problem facing the world. The populations of each country must be limited according to area and resources available. Strict Population control programs must be imposed. The one child policy of China is a classic example of controlling population. This can be implemented in other countries as well.

Countries like India, Pakistan, Bangladesh, Indonesia need to implement strict population control policy. There are millions of people in these countries struggling for food every day, due to overpopulation. More population means more struggle for food , economic opportunity, more de-forestation and causes of terrorism increase many times. Countries with huge population develop slowly, whatever development the government makes, the population will nullify the same.

Chapter 35

RESPONSIBILITY OF YOUTH – ONE CHILD POLICY OR NO CHILD POLICY.

The youth all over the world has the responsibility, either adopt one child policy or no child policy. Just imagine, if you bring a new person to earth, how much resources he is going to consume right from birth to death. Imagine a person is going to live up to 60 years:

Oxygen consumed:

Meat consumed:

Wheat/rice consumed:

Vegetables/packed food consumed:

Clothes/plastic/steel/paper used:

Carbon Die oxide emitted:

Water consumed:

Have you ever thought about it ? If no, here are some statistics. Don't be shocked. It is a reality.

A person breathes 7 or 8 liters of air per minute. Air is about 20% oxygen. But when you exhale, your breath is about 15% oxygen, so you consumed about 5%. Therefore, a person uses about 550 liters of pure oxygen each day. So a person consume 550 litres x 365 x 60 = 12045000 litres of oxygen, if he is alive for 60 years. If one million births can be controlled as per idea of no child policy, we save 12045000 litres of oxygen x 1,00,0000 = **12045000000000 litres of oxygen. This is a massive quantity.**

"One acre of trees annually consumes the amount of carbon dioxide equivalent to that produced by driving an average car for 26,000 miles. That same acre of trees also produces enough oxygen for 18 people to breathe for a year." - New York Times.

In a nutshell, if you do not produce a baby, it is equivalent to planting hundreds of tress.

Chapter 36

MEAT CONSUMPTION.

The USDA estimate of US per capita loss-adjusted meat consumption was 62.6 kg (138 lb). So, if you do not produce a kid, you are going to save hundreds of cattle and livestock in future. Assume average weight of 1 cattle is 700kg, a 60 year old person consume, 62.6 kg x 60 = 3756 kg of meat = 5.3 Cattle in a life time.

This is a very low estimate, actually a person in America consume more than 10 cattle weight 700kg in his life time, The consumption of meat in Middle east countries are much higher. As a rough estimate a meat eating person eat 10 cattle in his life time, if one million people do not have kids, we save 100 million cattle. Cattle population is one of the main cause of global warming because they emit methane.

Chapter 37

THROW AWAY GOLD AND DIAMONDS.

Can you take a decision today, I won't wear gold and diamond or any metal jewelry. When someone wear gold or diamonds as jewelry, somewhere in the world more people are digging mines and destroying the environment. If people like you refuse to wear gold and diamonds, the mines will soon close down and there won't be no more mining and destruction of environment. Even a single person can make a big impact. When millions of people decide to abandon jewelry, the results will be awesome. You can live without jewelry, actually you don't need it.

Chapter 38

CONCLUSION.

I have decided to write this book, only to make people understand that you can prevent terrorism and destruction of this world, if you want to do so. Every decision you take affects the world. Your impact may me tiny, but when million people like you take decisions to control your thinking and control world population, we create a better tomorrow. This is critical to save the future of our generations to come. Entering into any terror organization and working for them, will not bring peace, you will eventually meet death. This is like mafia, once you enter, you will not be able to come out. Please donate this book to anyone with extreme views, I am sure he will mellow down a bit. All the best

Warm Regards

GIJO VIJAYAN

Kochi, Kerala State
Republic of India

ABOUT THE AUTHOR

Mr. Gijo Vijayan is a serial entrepreneur based in India. A former student of **Sainik School,Kazhakootam, Kerala, one of the premier military schools in INDIA**. This book was written after studying and observing terrorism and activities of various organizations over many years. The author aims at exposing the truth about terrorism to public so that nobody get trapped into it and get killed eventually. So many misguided youth like fire flies embrace the flame of militancy and die young leaving their families in peril. Guns will not solve the problems of the world, commonsense and negotiations can solve even very big problems. This book will be an eye opener for all those with extreme ideologies, who want to take up guns. **Always remember that TERRORISM IS THE ENEMY OF HUMANITY.**